CLEVER COSTUME CREATING

for Halloween

"Halloween is a fun holiday that appeals to all ages. This book makes it possible for anyone to create an original and wearable costume, using materials generally found in the household. The fact that the costumes are so easy to make, using the directions and descriptions, means that participation in the holiday will be easier than ever."

~ The Halloween Association

CLEVER COSTUME CREATING
for Halloween

an A to Z guide of 200 costume ideas

Suzanne Singleton

Twenty-Nine
Angels
Publishing

P.O. Box 907
Sparks, Maryland 21152

410.771.4821
410.472.3204 - fax
twentynineangels@aol.com

Clever Costume Creating for Halloween

The information in this book is presented in good faith, however, no warranty is given, nor results guaranteed. Since the publisher has no control over physical conditions surrounding the applications of this information, the publisher and author disclaim any liability for untoward results. All efforts have been made to ensure the accuracy of the content. We cannot, however, be responsible for human error, interpretation, or variations of individual work. Ideas presented in this book are not intended to hurt, insult, or offend any individual, group, organization, nationality, religion or profession.

FIRST EDITION

10 9 8 7 6 5 4 3 2 1

Singleton, Suzanne.
Clever Costume Creating for Halloween. Summary: an A to Z guide of Halloween costume ideas for all ages.

ISBN 0-9661253-3-9
Library of Congress Control Number: 00-090738

Acknowledgments

Big angel thanks to so many friends and family members who shared their clever ideas, pictures and two cents!

A hefty Halloween howl to all the comical, crazy, wacky, zany, kooky, hilarious, silly, witty and imaginative people who show up in Fells Point to celebrate Halloween . . . you all have truly mastered the Halloween spirit!

For Linda Ports . . . Working with a friend is tops! And working with you is smooth, comfortable and fun! Jumbo thanks for your super imagination and your gifted hand which give my ideas color and LIFE! I am thankful for you as an artist and as a lifelong friend. (I owe you pitchers and pitchers of rum punch for this one!)

Credits

Cover, illustrations and book design:
    Linda Ports
    LP Design & Visual Communications
    Perry Hall, Maryland

Editors:
    Bonnie Stecker
    Paula Molino
    Donna Babylon, author of *More Splash Than Cash Decorating Ideas*

Proofreaders:
    Susan Schmelz
    Gina Molino
    Margaret Gemmill

We invite you to share in the joy, spirit,
and peace of the angels by finding
all 29 of them throughout this book!

 # The Costumes

Halloween . . . what fun! It's not just for kids! Halloween provides an opportunity for our inner child to come out and play. At what other time are we allowed to play dress-ups? Isn't it fun to assume the character of someone or something else? Plenty of adults enjoy dressing in costume and hosting Halloween parties.

If you have children, you know how much time it can take and how tedious it can be to invent an original Halloween costume - one that makes the kids happy. By the time you finish assembling their costumes, there may be little time to create one for yourself. Let us help!

Clever Costume Creating offers 200 costume ideas, most of which are simple for you or your group to create. Many of them are constructed by putting together specific pieces of clothing and props found around the house or borrowed from a friend. There's no need to spend a bunch of money to create a good Halloween costume. Shop in clothing thrift stores and scan flea markets for low-cost costume pieces. Many of the props mentioned can be found in costume stores around Halloween. Or, ask around - someone has it, does it, stores it, saves it, or works on it. Most costumes listed in our A to Z guide require just a few basic materials such as foil, spray paint, cardboard, poster board, string, ribbon, foam board, or a box.

Some ideas may be more time consuming than others . . . it's up to you to take an idea as far as you want. Costume ideas do not have to be elaborate. Cute is good. Funny is great. Creative will inspire the comment, "Now why didn't I think of that?" All ideas are presented as good, clean, and wholesome fun to celebrate that silly, scary and wacky day of Halloween. So skim through this costume alphabet of 200 ideas for inexpensive, no-sew and clever costume ideas, from ANTS to ZOMBIES!

What are <u>you</u> going to be for Halloween?

1

The ABC's for a Smart, Safe & Happy Halloween
reminders and suggestions for kids and adults

Always trick or treat in familiar neighborhoods.

Be as comfortable as possible in costume.

Carry a flashlight while trick or treating.

Do not trick or treat at homes where the lights are off.

End the trick or treating at a reasonable hour. Latest suggested quitting time is 9:00 p.m. On the flip side, don't start too early ~ neighbors may not be ready. Earliest suggested starting time is 5:00 p.m.

Find the unwrapped candy in the trick or treat bag and toss it.

Give away half of the collected candy to the needy. Find out which schools or local organizations have programs which collect candy during the week after Halloween. The candy is donated to kids who didn't get the chance to celebrate Halloween because of illnesses or disabilities.

Hand out only individually wrapped candy.

In the foyer set up a small table with baskets of candy ready for trick or treaters. Plan for enough.
If new to a neighborhood, ask the neighbors ahead of time how many trick-or-treaters to expect.

Join in for trick or treating at a local mall instead of going door to door.

Kindly say "Trick or Treat" when the door opens, and "Thank You!" after people give treats.

Little ones should be chaperoned from door to door. Do not send small kids out alone.

Make costumes as comfortable as possible.

2

No messing up other people's property with soap, toilet paper or smashed pumpkins.

Older kids should not trick or treat. Parents should decide what is "too old". The suggested age is 13. After that, teens can hand out the treats instead of collecting them. If teens are going to trick or treat, at least wear costumes! Older kids could chaperone little siblings or neighborhood kids and still participate in the process.

Parents could drive kids house to house if homes are too spread apart.

Quantity is not the goal! Go slow while trick or treating to stay safe and polite.

Respect people's property. Do not trample on small bushes, flowers and on lighting. Use walkways and driveways.

Stay on sidewalks when walking from house to house instead of walking in the street.

Take off masks before driving a car.

Use common sense - if wearing a bulky or large costume, put it on after arriving at a party. Be smart and safe when dressing in costume. Do not wear a costume that will impair vision or movement, especially when driving.

Very responsible people do not drink alcohol at Halloween parties and then drive afterwards.

Walk around with at least two other people while trick or treating.

X-cite the kiddies! Decorate the front door and steps with fun Halloween decor. Dress in costume while handing out the goodies.

Your Halloween party for children and their friends should not be on Halloween night. Kids may rather go trick or treating. Unless trick or treating is part of the party, plan the festivities for another evening. Consider having it a night or two after Halloween when it's less hectic for most families and the hype of Halloween night is over.

Zip around quicker in a lawn tractor with a pull wagon, or a golf cart. These are perfect vehicles to take kids trick or treating in a large neighborhood.

A is for ANTS

WEAR: brown sweatsuits, brown gloves

MAKE: antennae from a headband and brown pipe cleaners; oversized cardboard picnic items out of colored foam board such as an olive, wedge of cheese, slice of watermelon, a grape (purple balloon)

PROPS: red/white checkered tablecloth, large picnic basket, oversized ant spray

Others in the group can dress as a PICNIC (see P), a BASKET, ANT SPRAY, or WATERMELON

AUTOGRAPH HOUND

WEAR: white sweats with hooded sweatshirt, white mittens, white socks over shoes; write autographs all over costume; have people at the party "sign" you!

MAKE: floppy hound dog ears, tail

PROPS: red dog collar, oversized marker

AUTO MECHANIC

WEAR: a gray or tan jumpsuit; add lettering on the back, i.e., "Ken's Auto Shop", sneakers, smear grease on face and hands

PROPS: carry a toolbox, motor oil, or a car part like a generator or piece of fender; put tools and dirty rags in pockets

AVIATOR

WEAR: bomber jacket, scarf around neck, khaki pants, high boots, goggles, leather flight helmet (with flaps over ears)

PROP: toy airplane or glider

ASTRONAUT

WEAR: blue or orange jumpsuit with NASA or USA written across back and on front pocket; baseball hat with NASA on it

PROPS: toy rocket, or make a large cardboard rocket

7

B is for BLACK SHEEP   BAG LADY

WEAR: layers of raggy clothes, torn shoes with holes, head scarf tied under chin, old lady mask or smudged face, loose stockings, gloves

PROPS: toy (or real) grocery cart, stuffed plastic grocery bags, tin cup. Set up in a corner of the party with a cardboard box, tattered blanket and a rug.

WEAR: black fleece hooded sweatsuit, black mittens, paint black nose and large black eyelashes, black shoes

MAKE: sheep ears and a tail (pipe cleaner inside material)

PROPS: three bags labeled "for Master", "for Dame", "for Little Boy"

BANDITO

WEAR: sombrero, torn shorts, torn white long sleeved shirt, serape from shoulder to opposite hip, flip flops or sandals, white socks, mustache

PROPS: tequila, guitar

BEAUTY QUEEN

<u>WEAR:</u> evening gown, sash with state's name, tiara, rhinestone jewelry, white evening gloves, high heels
<u>PROP:</u> flowers

An alternate idea is to do a BEAUTY QUEEN SPOOF by dressing up as a beauty queen from a specific town in the area. Props can be things indicative of the town or county (e.g., stuffed toy cow for a farming community).

BIKER

WEAR: jeans, leather jacket, motorcycle logo on T-shirt, leather chaps, bandana around head, black boots, black gloves, tattoos; a guy can wear one earring and beard; a girl can wear tight pants, leather vest over a camisole

the BLUES BOYS

BROTHERHOOD
Society Members

WEAR: sunglasses, dark blue or black suits, black hats, dress shoes, white shirts and black ties

PROPS: microphones, saxophones

WEAR: black bow tie, white dress shirt, maroon suit jacket, gray dress pants

MAKE: hat out of maroon hard felt, add tassel

BUBBLE BATH

<u>WEAR:</u> white clothes, slippers, bare shoulders, pin white pearlized balloons to clothing, shower cap or put up hair

<u>MAKE:</u> small bathtub out of white poster board or cardboard box. Use aluminum foil to make a faucet; strands of curling ribbon coming out of faucet to simulate water

<u>PROPS:</u> shower brush, white towel, rubber duck, candles

BURGLAR

<u>WEAR:</u> black clothing, woman's nylon over face, or ski mask or a black mask over eyes, black gloves, pageboy hat or knit hat, black jacket

<u>PROPS:</u> toy gun, flashlight, sack of loot containing jewelry, candlesticks, silver, small electronics

13

BUTT-CRACK WORKMAN

<u>WEAR:</u> white tank shirt, construction boots, jeans with white underwear sticking out of the back. Pull pants down as far as needed to show butt crack, or use a fake butt

<u>PROPS:</u> red bandana and plumbing tools hanging out of back pocket, toolbox, plunger

C is for CANDY DOTS

WEAR: king-size white pillow case (cut open sides and cut hole for head), cover in 3-inch styrofoam balls (cut in half) painted in bright colors and hot glued in rows, or use large pompoms found in craft stores. Wear polka-dotted pants and shirt.

CAPTAIN TREASURE

WEAR: pirate costume and hat, gold jewelry, mustache, long black wig, high white socks, black shoes with buckles

PROPS: sword, treasure chest, parrot, boot-leg whiskey bottle, bag of gold coins

COMPUTER BUG

WEAR: a bug costume, or a shirt or pajamas with bugs all over, antennae

PROPS: a cardboard computer screen on a string around neck, a cardboard keyboard (or carry a real one)

CEREAL KILLER

WEAR: black clothes

PROPS: an empty cereal box on a string around neck, stab a fake knife in the center of box, add fake blood near punctured area

For a scarier version - wear all black clothes, black stocking over face or a scary mask, and a black cape with a hood. Attach miniature, empty cereal boxes all over cape. Carry a fake bloody knife.

16

CATNAP

CHARACTERS

Dress up like a favorite character from a television show, movie, cartoon, fairy tale, or nursery rhyme, or as a celebrity or sports player.

<u>WEAR:</u> pajamas, cat slippers, ears, whiskers, tail, black nose, mittens

<u>PROPS:</u> alarm clock, pillow, blanket

17

CHAP

WEAR: black suit, black hat, bowtie, stubby mustache, bushy eyebrows, large shoes

PROP: walking cane

CIGARETTE GIRL

WEAR: short skirt, low-cut frilly blouse, high heels, fishnet stockings, thick makeup, coiffed hair

MAKE: plastic tray with straps (use a drawer organizer or shallow cardboard box)

PROPS: inside of tray: cigarettes, cigars, gum, mints, lip balm, candy, small cup of coins

18

CIRCUS PERFORMERS

CHARACTERS:

Ring Leader - red tuxedo jacket with tails, white tuxedo shirt, red bow tie, black top hat, black pants, bushy mustache, microphone

Trapeze Artist - sequined leotard, tights, ballerina slippers, sequined crown or tiara, long hair or braid

Clown - large, colorful, mismatched clothes, colorful wig, clown makeup, red nose, clown shoes, balloons, horn

Lion Tamer - khaki knickers, white shirt, construction boots, safari jacket, whip, safari hat, stuffed lion or tiger

Very Short Person - see V

19

CLOTHESLINE

WEAR: clothespin bag on one person; laundry basket on other

MAKE: string a clothesline between two people; attach underwear, socks, and clothing (baby clothes are smaller and lighter)

PROPS: clothespins, birds on heads

COACH

WEAR: warmup suit, or sweatpants and windbreaker with name of school on back, whistle on string around neck, sneakers, baseball cap with school logo

PROPS: clipboard and pen, stopwatch, scorebook, basketballs or soccer balls in mesh bag

CHIMNEY SWEEPER

WEAR: dark clothing, vest, scarf at neck, black smudges on face and hands, pageboy hat or go formal with black suit and top hat

PROPS: broom, paint a cardboard smoke stack to resemble bricks and glue cotton smudged with soot at top of chimney

21

COOKIES and MILK

Chocolate Chip - tan sweatsuit, glue dark brown felt circles or brown buttons or pompoms all over

Chocolate Creme - white tights, shorts, and shirt; make cookie from black foam board (one for front; one for back) and wear over shoulder with ribbon or elastic straps

Vanilla Wafer - white tights, shorts, and shirt; make oblong vanilla wafer from tan foam board for front/back

Gingerbread - light brown sweatsuit; using fabric paint, draw white lines in zigzag pattern along arms and legs to "outline" the cookie, or hot glue white rickrack

Cookie Box or Jar - decorate a large cardboard box with holes cut for arms and head; write COOKIES on it

Milk Carton - simulate a cardboard milk carton shape out of white cardboard; write the verbiage from a real milk carton - nutritional contents, etc.

CRAZY NURSE

<u>WEAR:</u> torn and sloppy nurse uniform smeared with fake blood (ketchup, red food coloring), torn white pantyhose, sneakers with crazy design shoelaces, wild makeup, dark circles under eyes, blacked out tooth, askew nurse cap, teased hair, bandaids on face and neck, ace bandage around knee

<u>MAKE:</u> a giant needle out of cardboard

<u>PROPS:</u> medical bag, enema, stethoscope

CHRISTMAS ORNAMENT

<u>WEAR:</u> angel wings, halo, white dress or gown

<u>MAKE:</u> oversized ornament hook out of floral wire and attach to halo

<u>PROP:</u> harp

A group can dress as GLASS ORNAMENTS. Cut shapes (sphere, star, bell, etc.) from cardboard and decorate with paint and glitter. Cover hat boxes with silver foil and attach hooks.

CUPID

<u>WEAR:</u> red diaper or boxer shorts with hearts, short curly wig, red lipstick, heart tattoos, angel wings; red lipstick kisses and small red hearts all over face

<u>PROPS:</u> bow and arrow, give out candy hearts from a red bag tied around waist

D is for DALMATIAN

WEAR: white sweats with hooded sweatshirt, white gloves, paint face white with black spots, black nose

MAKE: tail, dog ears on hood, attach black felt spots to sweatsuit or draw with black fabric marker

PROPS: red leash or dog collar around neck, dog bone, firefighter's hat

Partner can be a FIREFIGHTER - see T for Transportation

DEPARTMENT STORE SHOPPING BAG

WEAR: turtleneck, tights, shorts

MAKE: cut off top and bottom flaps of cardboard box. Cut out holes for arms. Cover box in white or brown paper; draw logo on front and back. Attach handles from real shopping bag onto top of box, or use twine stiffened with glue. Attach straps of ribbon over shoulders to keep bag in place. Secure tissue paper sticking out of top of bag. Staple a large receipt onto tissue or make a hairbow out of a long receipt and attach "50% off" or "sale" tags to it with pipe cleaners.

DECK of CARDS

<u>WEAR:</u> black clothing

<u>MAKE:</u> playing cards (one card per person) with white poster board to indicate poker hand (i.e., three of a kind, four of a kind, royal flush). To make card backs, cover poster board in a thin red or blue patterned fabric or gift wrap. Attach front and back to bodies using ribbon or suspenders over shoulders.

Another person could dress as a CARD DEALER.

E is for EACH OTHER

<u>WEAR:</u> Simulate the look of a spouse or partner with clothing, wigs, mustache, makeup, etc. Wear each other's clothes or those of his/her job or hobby such as golfer, shopper, sports nut, aerobics instructor, banker.

<u>PROPS:</u> whatever is indicative of spouse (can of beer, remote control, apron, broom, etc.)

EGYPTIAN

WEAR: white sarong around waist (or use a tennis skirt), bare chest, gold fabric bands around wrists and ankles, sandals, white head wrap, chunky gold necklace with fake gems, bold rings, black eyeliner which extends beyond corners of eyes

(Female can wear a long, white, sleeveless and belted empire-waist dress)

ERA

WEAR: fashions representative of a selected era, such as 1920's - flappers . . . 1930's - gangsters . . . 1940's - World War II . . . 1950's - poodle skirts and greasers . . . 1960's - hippies and flower power . . . 1970's - disco, etc.

27

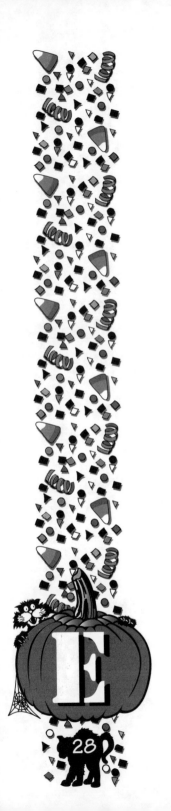

ELF

<u>WEAR:</u> green and red apron, suspenders, tights, shorts, and red or green striped turtleneck

<u>MAKE:</u> red and green pointy ears and hat cut from felt, or Santa hat, elf shoes with bells

<u>PROPS:</u> bells on long ribbon around neck, candy canes, sack labeled "toys"

Partner can dress up as SANTA or MRS. CLAUS, or TOY SOLDIER (see T)

F is for FADS

What are the crazes and fads of today and yesterday? Hula hoops, mood rings, new wave, punk rockers, pet rocks, cabbage patch dolls . . . incorporate a fad into a costume in a comical way.

FISHERMAN

<u>WEAR:</u> hip boots, fisherman's hat, camouflage clothes or plaid flannel shirt

<u>PROPS:</u> tackle box, fake fish or old boot on end of a fishing pole

29

FIGHTER and BOXING RING ASSISTANT

ROUND 3

WEAR: long open robe, elastic waist sport shorts, soft shoes or wrestling shoes, white socks, towel around neck, large ski mittens or boxing gloves, black eye, fake bruises, bloody lip

PROP: small 3-legged stool

Boxing Ring Assistant - sexy clothes, high heels, hold a sign which reads 'ROUND 3'

G is for GANGSTER

WEAR: pin-striped dark suit, dark dress shirt, white tie, brimmed hat

PROPS: flower in lapel, skinny mustache, sideburns, toy gun, cigarette or cigar

GARBAGE BAG or CAN

WEAR: garbage bag stuffed with paper, or use a plastic garbage can with a lid; cut out bottom, put lid on head; attach empty cans, milk cartons and other trash

PROPS: Smear face with real catsup and mustard (or use face paint), hang stuffed raccoon from side or attach to lid

31

GAUDY GIRL

GIANT

WEAR: leopard skin-tight pants, wild and gaudy clothes (animal prints work well), cover face and arms with dark tanning cream (or dark foundation) to simulate tan, thick colorful makeup

PROPS: gaudy accessories: large purse, big jewelry, scarf, sunglasses, hat, funky shoes

WEAR: pants which are too short, long sleeve shirt too short on arms, platform shoes, bangs combed forward; for a green giant - paint arms, legs and face/neck

PROPS: miniature dollhouse items and people

GHOST WRITER

WEAR: white sheet over entire body with holes cut out for eyes and mouth, write sentences and poetry all over sheet with a black marker

PROPS: oversized pencil

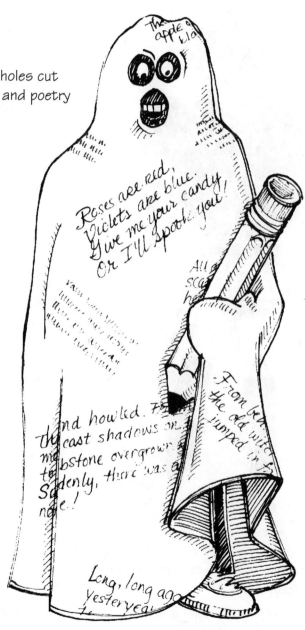

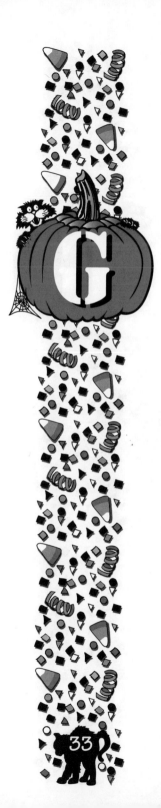

GRAPES

GROCERY BAG

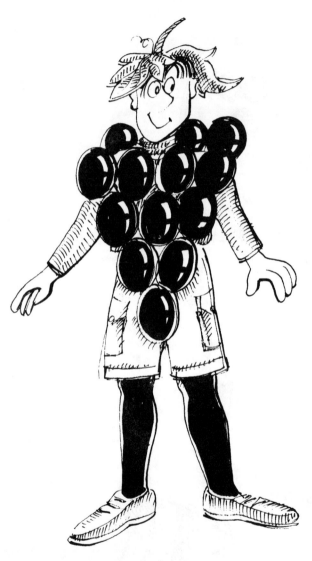

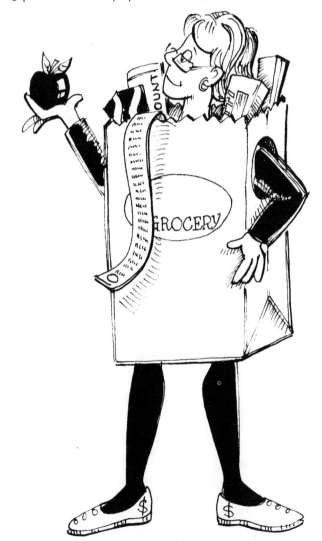

WEAR: brown sweats, or brown tights and turtleneck

MAKE: write a grocery store name on a cardboard box; zigzag the top. Attach empty products to top of box such as boxes from cereal, rice, spaghetti, cookies and bottles from detergent and soda; make receipt out of long piece of white paper and hang it over the side.

WEAR: purple (or green) turtleneck and shorts, brown tights, pin dark purple (or green) balloons on torso in form of bunch of grapes

MAKE: brown felt pointy hat for the stem

*Partner could be a **WEDGE of CHEESE** - see Ants*

GYPSY FORTUNE TELLER

<u>WEAR:</u> lots of gaudy costume jewelry (earrings, bracelets, necklaces), heavy makeup, colorful long gauze skirt, off shoulder peasant blouse, bright sash around waist, bandana around head, long wig or teased hair, bare feet or sandals, toe rings, ankle bracelets

<u>PROPS:</u> crystal ball, tarot cards

35

H is for HALF-MAN/HALF-WOMAN

This can be done two ways: 1) front and back or 2) side by side.

<u>WEAR:</u> cut all clothes and accessories in half: sew half of man's shirt/pants to half of woman's shirt/skirt. Wear half a hat, makeup on half of face, use half a wig, one earring, one hand with fingernail polish and jewelry, one man's shoe, one woman's shoe, etc.

To be very creative, try a theme.
See couple ideas throughout book:

Quarterback and Cheerleader

Salt and Pepper

Nun and Priest

Queen and King

Each Other

HIPPIE

WEAR: 60's or 70's clothes: hipster pants, fringed vests, long gauze skirt, T-shirt with 60's/70's rock band logo, raggy jeans with ripped knees, peace sign and flowers embroidered or painted on jeans, long stringy wig, small round sunglasses, tattoos, long beads around neck, choker necklaces, ring on each finger, tie bandana across forehead, sandals, beards, sideburns, and goatees

PROPS: bong, lava lamp, incense, duffel bag, guitar, "Make Love Not War" sign

HOLLYWOOD MOVIE STAR

WEAR: evening gown or tuxedo, dark glasses, fur coat, feather boa, top hat, cane

PROP: gold "Oscar" statue

Partner can be a LIMO DRIVER - see T for Transportation

H

HOBBIES

CHARACTER IDEAS:

Artist	Gardener	Motorcyclist	Sports Nut
Baseball Card Collector	Golfer	Photographer	Softball Player
Chef	Horseback Rider	Pilot (see Aviator)	Snorkler
Cyclist	Ice Skater	Rollerblader	Swimmer (see Pool Pal)
Fisherman (see F)	Jogger	Skier	Tennis Player

I is for IVY TRELLIS

WEAR: all green, rig a piece of white plastic trellis behind head; attach lots of plastic ivy strands up, down and around body

ISLAND GIRL

WEAR: grass skirt, coconut bra, black long-haired wig, flower in hair, lei, sandals or bare feet . . . and do the hula dance!

ITALIAN DINNER and WAITER

MAKE: cut head hole in middle of foam board. Cover with red/white checkered fabric or paper tablecloth, long enough to reach knees. "Set table" by hot gluing miniatures of wine, vase of flowers, napkins, paper plates, plastic utensils, fake spaghetti (red string) and meatballs (red styrofoam balls) on plate, small cheese container, bread, salad (torn up green tissue paper) etc.

Waiter - black tuxedo (or white shirt, black pants), white napkin over arm, wine list, corkscrew, pepper grinder, menu

J is for JACK BE NIMBLE

WEAR: knickers, white socks pulled up to knee, vest, white frilly shirt, newsboy hat, shoes with buckles

PROPS: candlestick

Group idea: Mother Goose and nursery rhyme characters like Little Bo Peep, Humpty Dumpty, Jack Horner.

JUDGE

WEAR: black judge's robe or graduation gown, pearls, bifocal glasses, tan pantyhose, black conservative shoes, short brown wig

PROPS: gavel, law book

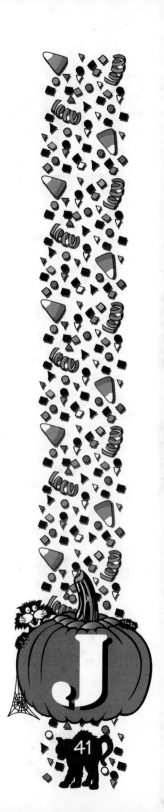

K is for KUNG FU MASTER and STUDENT

WEAR: karate outfit with black belt, bald skull cap, create slanted eyes with makeup, wooden thong sandals, fu-man-chu mustache and beard (gray and stringy)

PROPS: bamboo stick

Student - white karate outfit, yellow karate belt

L is for LAUNDRY BASKET

LOST & FOUND

WEAR: round laundry basket, cut hole in bottom to fit around waist; inside place crumpled clothes, towels, socks, box of detergent

Two other people can be a CLOTHESLINE (see C)

MAKE: Cardboard box labeled "lost and found" with items sticking out such as a mitten, an earring, a shoe, scarf, sweater, sock

43

LEPRECHAUN

<u>WEAR:</u> green tights, shorts and turtleneck, black blazer a size too small, black shoes with large rectangular gold buckles (painted cardboard), green beard, black top hat (plastic New Year's Eve hat) with green band and shamrocks all over, green scarf wrapped around neck

<u>PROPS:</u> pot of gold filled with gold-wrapped chocolate coins, poster board rainbow on a stick

LITTER of PUPPIES

WILL BEG FOR

<u>WEAR:</u> brown, black, and white fleece sweatsuits with hoods (or dye adult-size footy pajamas color of choice), paint black noses, mittens, wear socks of same color over shoes

<u>MAKE:</u> attach ears of stiff felt to hoods, use fake fur and two-sided sticky tape to make spots

<u>PROPS:</u> bones, dog bowl, dog toys

M is for MAILBOX with ENVELOPES

Mailbox - paint a tall cardboard box blue; cut out holes for arms and head, make a drop slot in the front. Write U.S. MAIL in white letters across front.

Envelopes - white foam board; write addresses and illustrate stamps; string them over the shoulders using wide white ribbon.

Addition to group: **MAIL CARRIER**- blue uniform including handmade U.S. MAIL logo on sleeve, blue cap with logo, mailbag, stuffed dog hanging onto butt or ankle.

Soccer Journal
1246 Goal Plaza
Score, MD 20012

MAD SCIENTIST

<u>WEAR:</u> white lab coat, sloppy clothes, dirty sneakers, frizzy hair or wear a messy wig, bags under eyes

<u>PROP:</u> beakers

MAGICIAN

<u>WEAR:</u> black pants, white shirt, red bow tie, black magician's hat, black cape

<u>PROPS:</u> stuffed rabbit, magician's wand, silk scarves tied together, magic tricks, magic bag

Partner can dress as MAGICIAN'S ASSISTANT

47

MAGNET

<u>WEAR:</u> all red clothes, gray gloves and shoes; attach items all over body that a magnet would attract: paper clips, nails, tacks, tin cans, earrings, wrench, hammer

<u>PROPS:</u> large magnet

MAMMY

<u>WEAR:</u> red/white polka dotted dress with puffed sleeves, dark leggings and leotard under dress, white bib apron, red bandana around head, gold hoop earrings, dark makeup on face

<u>PROPS:</u> baby doll, bottle, diaper pins, cloth diaper over shoulder

MR. ICE CREAM MAN

WEAR: all white clothes, white hat, coin belt

PROPS: fake ice cream on a stick or an empty box of popsicles; small dolls attached to legs (to simulate children)

MONK

WEAR: hooded long brown robe, rope belt, large cross on twine (make cross from stiff felt)
PROP: Bible

MONKEY BUSINESS

WEAR: business suit, tie, dress shoes, long curly monkey tail, monkey mask, fur over tops of hands or wear brown gloves

MAKE: palm tree on stick

PROP: briefcase, bunch of bananas

MOTHER'S AU PAIR

WEAR: hat with flowers, conservative suit with long jacket, pointy lace-up boots, cape

PROPS: umbrella, stroller, babydoll

N is for NERD

WEAR: pants too short, white socks, ugly shoes, out of style checkered blazer, white shirt, sloppy tie, glasses with tape on nose bridge, greased hair parted in the middle, unzipped fly with part of shirt pulled through zipper, fake buck teeth, smeared chocolate on mouth and chin

PROPS: many pencils and pens in pocket protector sticking out of jacket pocket, calculator

NERDY BASEBALL FAN

WEAR: team shirt or uniform, big shoes, pins and team buttons on hat, plastic nose/glasses, messy wig

PROPS: scorebook, sports books, baseball, autograph book and pen, baseball cards, large foam "#1" hand, small cooler

NERDY SCOUT

NERDY TOURIST

WEAR: white blouse, green or blue pants or skirt, sash, saddle shoes, green knee-high socks with tassels, nerdy glasses with tape on nose bridge, pigtails, shirt hanging out of pants

PROPS: handbook, box of cookies

WEAR: Hawaiian print shirt, Bermuda shorts, sandals with white socks, straw hat, sunglasses

PROPS: camera and video camera on straps around neck, vacation pamphlets and brochures sticking out of shirt and back pockets, beachy tote bag, white sunblock on nose

NIGHT

WEAR: all black or navy blue clothing or long gown, glue on glow-in-the-dark stars, paint face with stars and moon

MAKE: crown of stars (use the silver strand of stars on a wire used to decorate Christmas trees)

PROPS: white cardboard crescent moon or star

NUN and PRIEST

NUN: long black robe, large crucifix around neck, black veil with stiff white piece of cardboard across forehead

PRIEST: black shirt and pants, crucifix around neck, stiff white collar

PROPS: Bible, holy water, rosary, goblet

53

O is for OLD FASHIONED HOUSEWIFE

ONE NIGHT STAND

<u>WEAR:</u> box covered with contact paper that looks like wood; cut out hole for head; paper doily glued around hole; attach to top of box: soda can, small lamp, jewelry box, bra, book; wear a lamp shade on head, illustrate drawers on the front of the box

<u>WEAR:</u> conservative shirtwaist dress with full skirt, pearls, white gloves, apron, high heeled pumps, pillbox hat, cardigan sweater with sweater clip, vintage clip earrings, hair in a bun, stiff bangs

<u>PROPS:</u> short-handled purse on arm, cat-eye glasses on chain

54

P is for PAINTED SPORTS FANS

<u>WEAR:</u> jeans, sweats or uniform pants; paint one letter of the name of a sports team on each person's chest; paint faces using team colors

<u>PROPS:</u> beer, pennants, team hats, "# 1" foam hand signs, peanuts, popcorn, scorebooks

PARACHUTIST

<u>WEAR:</u> gray jumpsuit, goggles, pilot's hat, stuffed nylon backpack

<u>MAKE:</u> cover a small umbrella with nylon; place handle down the back. Attach strings from umbrella to body to simulate parachute.

PICNIC

<u>WEAR:</u> red and white checked fabric (same fabric design is also available with black ants printed on it), bucket of chicken on head

<u>MAKE:</u> napkin and condiment necklace: punch holes in plastic mustard and ketchup containers and string together with red gimp; glue on paper plates and cups and plastic utensils

Partners can be ANTS (see A)

POOL PAL

WEAR: swimming trunks, flippers, animal inner tube around waist, swim mask and snorkel, bathing cap, water wings

PROPS: beach ball, suntan lotion

P.J. PARTY

<u>WEAR:</u> funny or cute pajamas, robes, character slippers, ponytails and pigtails, freckles, curlers in hair

<u>PROPS:</u> stuffed animals, diaries, pillows (have pillow fights)

Q is for QUARTERBACK and CHEERLEADER

QUEEN and KING

QUARTERBACK **(female):** football uniform and helmet, spikes, carry football, black under eyes

CHEERLEADER **(male):** sweater with varsity letter, short skirt, pigtails, sneakers or saddle shoes with bobby socks, small pompoms on shoes, carry pompoms or megaphone

A third person can be a POMPOM GIRL or MASCOT

<u>WEAR:</u> long capes bordered with white fur, bold jewelry; long full dress belted for queen; tights and knickers for king, beard

<u>MAKE:</u> tiara for queen; gold crown with large, colored gems for king

<u>PROP:</u> gold scepters

R is for RAINBOW

WEAR: each person dresses from head to toe in one rainbow color, wear mittens or gloves of same color, paint face same color or paint rainbow on cheeks, put socks of same color over shoes

PROPS: cardboard clouds, pot of gold

RED RIDING HOOD, WOLF, GRANDMOTHER, and WOODSMAN

Red Riding Hood - hooded red cape, white blouse, black or red skirt, red shoes, anklet socks, carry basket

Grandmother - conservative long nightgown, crocheted shawl around shoulders, slippers, granny cap, granny glasses

Woodsman - flannel shirt, jeans, construction boots, baseball cap, beard, ax

Wolf - wolf mask, jeans, shirt, cover hands and feet in fur

61

ROAD

WEAR: black clothes, black gloves

MAKE: Attach yellow or white ribbon to clothes (up/down the arms, legs, torso) to indicate lanes. Attach miniature toy cars and trucks, miniature stop, yield and street signs, and traffic lights. Attach a "road kill" animal using a shredded stuffed animal smeared with fake blood.

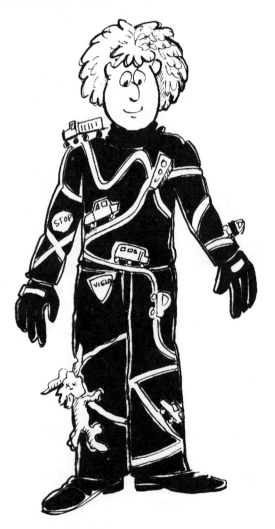

ROMAN

WEAR: white or blue toga (sheet wrapped around body; one bare shoulder), gold jewelry, head wreath of gold artificial leaves, gold rope belted at waist, sandals, gold cuff on upper arm

S is for SAFARI HUNTER   SALT & PEPPER

<u>WEAR:</u> khaki shorts, rope belt, animal print or khaki shirt, or tan fishing vest with lots of pockets, pith helmet, construction boots, mustache

<u>PROPS:</u> stuffed animals (leopard, elephant, tiger), toy rifle, canteen on belt, binoculars on neck, compass, maps, duffel bag

<u>WEAR:</u> one person wears all white clothing; the other wears all black

<u>MAKE:</u> shaker tops out of round hat boxes covered with foil; punch appropriate holes in top. Make "S" and "P" out of colored felt and attach to shirt fronts.

63

SANDWICH

<u>WEAR:</u> colored tights, shorts and shirt to match food color

Bread - cut two pieces of white foam in the shape of bread slices; color outer edges tan (for crust). Make wide ribbon straps to fit over shoulders. Make a large olive on a toothpick and attach to bread

Lettuce - glue pieces of wrinkled, dark green tissue paper on cardboard

Pickle - green foam board or painted cardboard in the shape of a dill pickle slice

Bologna - pink foam board or painted cardboard in a circular shape

Cheese - yellow foam board or painted cardboard with holes cut throughout to simulate Swiss cheese

Tomato - red foam board or painted cardboard in circular shape; draw lines and seeds to simulate tomato slice

Everyone can also dress in WITCH costumes under the sandwich pieces to be "SANDWITCHES"

SCARECROW

SCHOOLTEACHER

WEAR: plaid flannel shirt, old raggy pants, rope belt, stuff clothes with real straw or natural color raffia (in craft stores); attach patches on shirt and pants, raggy wig, straw hat

PROP: crow on shoulder; place sticks down back and across arms inside clothing

WEAR: flat shoes, bun in hair, no makeup, pearl earrings, buttoned up blouse with a big long skirt, or a very loose conservative dress, bifocal glasses on chain, ABC sweater tied over shoulders

PROPS: handheld chalkboard with chalk, notebook, apple, pencils in holder and in hair

65

SHEIK

<u>WEAR:</u> long white (or striped) gown or sheet, piece of white sheet over head with a colored band around forehead, beard, sunglasses

<u>PROP:</u> oil, money

SIMPLE PIEMAN

<u>WEAR:</u> white baker's hat, white apron, knickers, vest, high white socks, black shoes with large silver buckles

<u>PROPS:</u> fake pie, rolling pin, measuring spoons

66

SIAMESE BABY TWINS

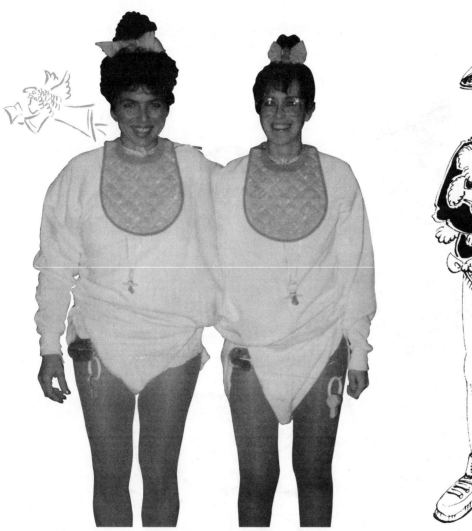

WEAR: bows or baby bonnets, saddle shoes or sneakers, lace socks, individual diapers with large baby pins, sheer pantyhose, bibs, pacifiers tied on ribbon around neck, pink blush on freckled cheeks, chocolate smeared on back of diapers

MAKE: cut off one arm of two sweatshirts and sew together

PROPS: baby bottles, teddy bears, diaper bags, baby toys

If you don't want to be attached, dress as TWINS.

67

SUMO WRESTLERS

<u>WEAR:</u> black headbands, flesh colored tights and flesh colored tight pullover shirts, wrap piece of sheet around buttocks to simulate a large diaper-like covering. Stuff outfits to simulate fat bodies. Black hair with high ponytails.

T is for
TACKY BRIDESMAID

TREE PEOPLE

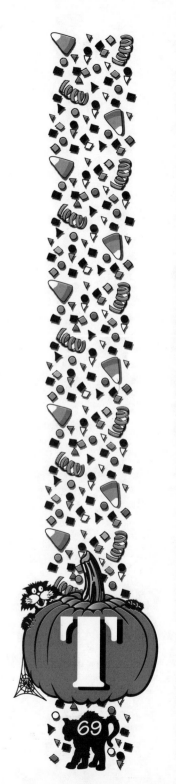

<u>WEAR:</u> ugly bridesmaid dress with big, gaudy bow; bra straps showing, knee-high stockings, overdone makeup, blue eye shadow, dyed shoes

<u>PROP:</u> wilted bouquet of flowers

<u>WEAR:</u> loin cloths, bare bodies (bathing suit top for Jane); stone or arrowhead on leather cord around necks, leaves in hair

<u>PROPS:</u> stuffed monkey, vines

69

THREE BLIND MICE

WEAR: gray sweats and hooded sweatshirts, white gloves, bow ties, plastic mouse noses or paint noses black

MAKE: mouse ears and attach to hoods, tails

PROPS: dowel sticks, dark glasses

A fourth group member can dress up as the FARMER'S WIFE - kerchief, housecoat, apron, rubber butcher knife

TATTOO FANATIC

WEAR: shorts and muscle shirt, apply fake tattoos all over legs and arms

TRUE SOUTHERN GENTLEMAN

WEAR: white suit, white shirt, white shoes, white wig, bushy white eyebrows, white Southern bow tie, white goatee, glasses

PROPS: cane, white hat

Partner can dress as a SOUTHERN BELLE

THREE WISE MEN

WEAR: long robes of regal colors (purple, gold, royal blue, red), beards

MAKE: gold pillbox hats with tassels

PROPS: gifts labeled "gold", "frankincense", "myrrh", walking sticks

TOOTH FAIRY

WEAR: short slip bordered with sequins or a fairy costume or white gown, wings, tights, ballet slippers

PROPS: tooth wand, bottle of stardust (silver confetti), large tooth or bag marked "teeth"

TOY SOLDIER

WEAR: marching band uniform, or navy blue pants with gold trim down sides and a red button-front shirt, gold epaulets, or a navy blue jacket with double breasted gold buttons, tall marching hat, white gloves, black shoes, mustache

PROPS: toy rifle, drum and drumsticks

73

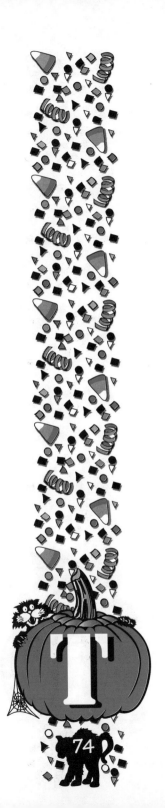

TRANSPORTATION

MAKE: Using four sides of cardboard box (remove top/bottom flaps), spray paint and decorate choice of transportation. Body will be inside as driver. Hold sides of box or make shoulder straps from suspenders or wide ribbon. Headlights can be created using small paper plates. Small aluminum pie plates can be used as hubcaps.

Taxicab	Race car	Bulldozer	Gondola
Police Car	Farm Tractor	Boat	Convertible
School Bus	Garbage Truck	Limousine	Mail Truck
Train	Fire Engine	Ambulance	

TRANSPORTATION (continued)

WEAR/PROPS:

Taxi Driver - casual clothes, cigar, baseball hat or pageboy cap, mustache

Police Officer - blue uniform, tall boots, badge, cap, nightstick, gun/holster, handcuffs, ticket book

Bus Driver - blue uniform or button down sweater or vest, cap, small stop sign

Engineer - jeans jacket, jeans, striped shirt, engineer's hat, red bandana on neck, train whistle

Race Car Driver - jumpsuit, helmet, put automotive stickers/endorsements all over cardboard car

Farmer - denim overalls, flannel shirt, straw hat, cardboard pitchfork, work boots

Garbage Collector - trash sticking out of clothes

Firefighter - red firefighter hat, yellow raincoat, rubber boots, hose, stuffed Dalmatian

Bulldozer Operator - white T-shirt, jeans, construction boots, hard hat, lunchbox

Boat Captain - swimsuit, T-shirt, sunblock, captain's hat (or see F for FISHERMAN)

Chauffeur - tuxedo or suit, chauffeur's cap, bottle of champagne

Paramedic - medical bag, stethoscope, medical symbol on navy blue uniform

Gondolier - red scarf around neck, black/white or red/white striped shirt, black pants, long pole

Convertible Driver - golf shirt, preppy pants, sunglasses, pipe or cigar

Mail Carrier - blue uniform including handmade U.S. MAIL logo on sleeve, blue cap with logo, mailbag, stuffed dog hanging onto butt or ankle

75

U is for
Miss UNIVERSE

<u>WEAR:</u> evening gown or one piece bathing suit, high heels, rhinestone jewelry, "Miss Universe" sash, tiara, lots of makeup and coiffed hair

<u>PROPS:</u> long stemmed roses, smile a lot!

UPSIDE DOWN PERSON

<u>WEAR:</u> gloves on feet, upside down shirt on bottom half of body (place legs inside shirt arms), upside down pants on the top half of body (cut out hole in seat of pants for face.) Pin or sew together shirt and pants. Attach fake head between knees and in the shirt collar to simulate person in handstand position. Stuff newspaper into pant legs to create bent knees. Attach stuffed socks to ends of pant legs.

V is for VERY SHORT PERSON

<u>WEAR:</u> shirt on lower body buttoned up to bellybutton. Stuff shirt arms and position into pants pockets. Pin shirt to pair of pants worn around your knees; secure with belt; roll up pants legs; pad seat of pants with small pillow to serve as buttocks. Place mask on belly, or draw face on bare stomach.

<u>MAKE:</u> oversized top hat out of black poster board to cover torso; cut holes on sides to free arms; cut out face hole. Attach long wig around back of waist.

77

VENTRILOQUIST

<u>WEAR:</u> identical clothes on ventriloquist and dummy

<u>PROPS:</u> dummy, small case for dummy

A second person could also dress and act as the DUMMY and sit in the lap of the ventriloquist. Cut a hole in the back of the shirt for the ventriloquist's hand. Paint lines on the person's face to indicate a talking mouth.

VODKA COCKTAIL

<u>WEAR:</u> clear, industrial-size garbage bag with holes cut in the bottom for legs (opening of bag will be at shoulders); attach opening of bag to a hula hoop or flexible, lightweight tubing; make shoulder straps from wide ribbon. Blown-up plastic sandwich bags serve as ice cubes and float loosely inside the bag around body.

<u>MAKE:</u> swizzle stick out of wrapping paper roll; stripe it with red ribbon or tape. For lemon or lime, twist piece of yellow or green fabric or fun foam and attach to shoulder to simulate it floating in the glass.

VOODOO DOCTOR

WEAR: black shirt and shorts, grass skirt (or make one using slit brown paper bag), war paint on face, wild black wig, skull necklace, sandals or bare feet

PROPS: cloth doll stuck with pins, burlap sack around waist

W is for WASHING MACHINE

WEAR: white clothes, white sneakers

MAKE: Spray paint a cardboard box white. Cut a hole in top of box for head and in front for door. Attach a piece of cardboard to serve as back of washer. For knobs, cover screw lids from empty detergent bottles with foil and label "hot", "cold", "delicates", etc. Cut two circles from clear mylar paper and place a few pieces of small clothing items in between (bra, socks, bunched up T-shirt). Glue together. Then glue the mylar circles to the inside of the cardboard box.

PROPS: empty bleach bottle and detergent box, measuring cup, dirty clothes

Partner can dress as a LAUNDRY BASKET (see L) or CLOTHESLINE (see C)

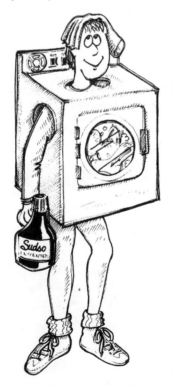

WATERMELON

WEAR: red tights, green turtleneck, green or red pants

MAKE: cut out a triangular shape from red foam board. Glue on "seeds" made from black construction paper. To simulate the "rind", glue a long piece of green construction paper along the bottom of the triangle. Attach this costume around the chest/back with a piece of elastic; hot glue the elastic to the foam board. Or, make two slices of watermelon for the front/back and put straps in between to wear over the shoulder.

Can go along with ANTS (see A) or PICNIC (see P)

WIND STORM

WEAR: business clothes, make ties and bottoms of jacket and dress stick out to one side (use starch or wire), put up collars, use gel to make hair stick out to one side

PROPS: inside-out umbrellas, askew newspapers, walk on an angle

Male could dress up as a female with skirt blowing up.

WIZARD

WEAR: purple cape with felt stars and moon, black clothing, long white beard

MAKE: cone hat (staple or glue stars/moon fabric to rolled poster board) or buy a felt hat

PROPS: sorcerer stick, magic book

X is for XTRAVAGANT RICH LADY

WEAR: evening wear or dressy business suit, feather boa or fur coat or mink stole with animal head, glitsy jewelry, several large gem rings, evening purse, excess makeup, white dress gloves

PROP: fake money

Partner can dress as CHAUFFEUR (see T for transportation)

Y is for YO-YO

MAKE: round red front and blue back from foam board; attach with wide ribbon over shoulders. Wrap string many times around waist; allow a long piece of string to hang down. Tie a loophole in end, or attach a plastic ring at end of string to serve as finger loop.

new YEAR'S eve baby

WEAR: black top hat with "Happy New Year", oversized diaper, sash across body announcing the new year

PROPS: noise maker, party blower, champagne bottle or flute

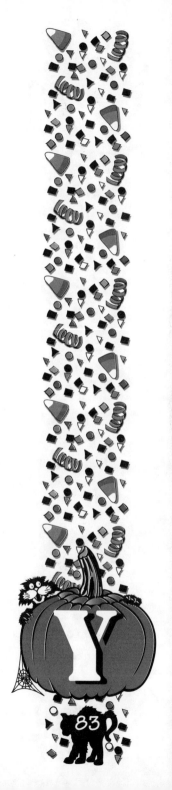

83

Z is for ZOMBIE

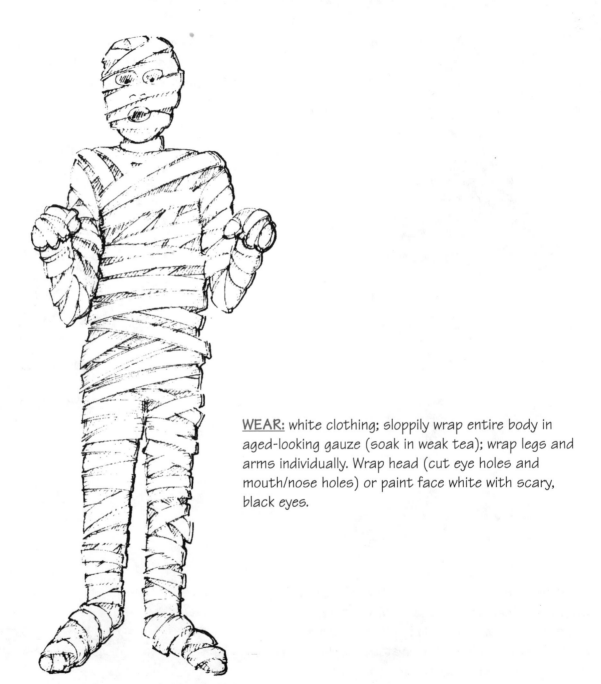

WEAR: white clothing; sloppily wrap entire body in aged-looking gauze (soak in weak tea); wrap legs and arms individually. Wrap head (cut eye holes and mouth/nose holes) or paint face white with scary, black eyes.

ZULU TRIBE

WEAR: black clothes, grass skirts (or make them using slit brown paper bags around waists) war paint on faces, wild black wigs

MAKE: cardboard shields with painted design, necklaces out of chicken bones and seashells, bamboo stick with fake skulls on top and hanging cornhusks

One person in the group can be dressed more elaborately as "The Chief"

85

Meet Suzanne . . .

Suzanne Molino Singleton established Twenty-Nine Angels Publishing, LLC in 1997 to produce her first book, *Clever Gift Giving*, the first in a series of "clever idea" titles. *Clever Costume Creating for Halloween* is her third title which follows *Clever Party Planning*, published in '99. Suzanne has plans for the growth of her company, including the publishing of three children's books which she has written. Several other completed books by Suzanne, including a novel, await their turn at production as Twenty-Nine Angels Publishing expands.

Suzanne creates from a home office in Maryland while nurturing two young kiddies and two twenty-something stepsons. Her husband is Ken Singleton, a baseball announcer for the New York Yankees and a former major leaguer (#29), mostly as a Baltimore Oriole.

Suzanne's life is greatly assisted by angels which is why she believes in them, collects them, talks to them, wears them, and includes them everywhere!

She thanks you wholeheartedly for buying this book!

Meet Linda . . .

Linda Ports of LP Design & Visual Communications is a freelance artist and graphic designer. She graduated with honors from the Art Institute of Pittsburgh with a degree in Visual Communications. After employment as a designer for an advertising agency and then as art director for a major corporation, Linda left the corporate world to freelance from a home studio while raising two sons and a daughter, now ages 13, 12 and 7.

The artist has designed numerous brochures, ads, posters, menus, murals, logos and corporate identity packages. Her work has been printed in newspapers, magazines and books. While Linda uses many mediums and styles of illustrating, she enjoys cartooning projects the best.

Linda has been married for 20 years to her high school sweetheart, Jim Ports. They are avid soccer enthusiasts who spend most of their spare time coaching and cheering for their kids who play in premiere leagues and tournaments up and down the east coast. Linda and Jim are co-owners of Sportsline, a silk screen/embroidery company that also sells trophies and equipment.

Linda thanks Suzanne for allowing her the opportunity to illustrate her creative books and especially for their long-time friendship. May there be many more rum punch cruises!

89

90

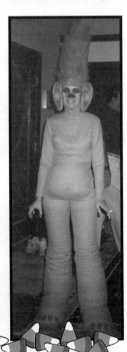

other titles by
Suzanne Singleton

and illustrated by
Linda Ports

Clever Gift Giving $9.95
ISBN 09661253-0-4, softcover, 80 pages

Give a unique gift that may be the hit of the party!
Over 300 fresh and clever ideas are yours for house-
warming, theme gifts, wedding shower, showing thanks,
giving to your teens and tots, and more! Packed with
inventive gift ideas, party tips, wrapping hints and
inspirational quotes. This whimsical handbook is guaranteed to jumpstart your creativity in gift giving!

Clever Party Planning $15.95
Theme Parties for kids, teens, and adults
ISBN 09661253-2-0, softcover, 208 pages

Organizing one of these clever 90 theme parties will be a
snap as Singleton provides detailed ideas and instruc-
tions for invitations, decorations, activities, games, con-
tests, crafts, treats, cakes, and party favors in this
complete party guide. Plan imaginative celebrations for
kids and adults, and the teens in-between!

To Order . . .

BY CREDIT CARD . . . call or e-mail (twentynineangels@aol.com) Twenty-Nine Angels Publishing @ 410-771-4821
or out of state @ 800-736-7729 during regular business hours (eastern time). Major credit cards accepted.

BY MAIL . . . send a check or money order payable to:
Twenty-Nine Angels Publishing, P.O. Box 907, Sparks, Maryland 21152

FREE SHIPPING when ordering directly from the publisher! Retail and library discount schedule is available.